TCR 9104

Kids Taking Action

READING COMPREHENSION

Real Kids Making Real Changes

Author
Tracy Edmunds, M.A. Ed.

Managing Editor
Mara Ellen Guckian

Editor in Chief
Brent L. Fox, M. Ed.

Creative Director
Sarah M. Fournier

Cover Artist
Diem Pascarella

Art Coordinator
Renée Mc Elwee

Illustrator
Renée Mc Elwee

Imaging
Crystal-Dawn Keitz

Publisher
Mary D. Smith, M.S. Ed.

Teacher Created Resources
12621 Western Avenue
Garden Grove, CA 92841
www.teachercreated.com

ISBN: 978-1-4206-1710-8

©2022 Teacher Created Resources

Made in U.S.A.

For standards correlations, visit
http://www.teachercreated.com/standards/

Teacher Created Resources

Table of Contents

Introduction 3

How to Use This Book 3

Community Investigation 5

Vocabulary List 7

Vocabulary Graphic Organizer 9

Taking Action 10

Unit 1: Christian Bucks 12

Unit 2: Aiden Wang 18

Unit 3: Garrett Lowry 24

Unit 4: A'Layah Robinson 30

Unit 5: Hailey Scheinman 36

Unit 6: Hana Fatima 42

Unit 7: Jane Velkovski 48

Unit 8: Jahkil Naeem Jackson 54

Unit 9: Samaira Mehta 60

Unit 10: Milo Cress 66

Unit 11: Gitanjali Rao 72

Motto Bookmarks 78

Bibliography 79

Introduction

Kids of all ages are eager to help build a better world. They see problems, in school and out. Many are concerned about both their immediate situations and their futures. They want to know what they can do to help.

Research shows that helping others relieves anxiety, reduces stress, improves mood, boosts self-esteem, and instills a sense of purpose and satisfaction. Taking positive actions can help kids cope with their fears and become informed, active citizens in their communities.

The informational texts in this book present examples of positive activism initiated by young people. The kids in these texts are "everyday people" making a difference in their communities through positive activism related to their environments, their education, and their desire to help people in need. They put their imaginations and optimism to work and truly make a difference. Their examples encourage students to find positive solutions and show them that their age is not a barrier to becoming forces for positive change.

> "Young people, when they understand a problem, are empowered to take action. When we listen to their voices (they) actually are changing the world and making it better for people, for animals, and for the environment because everything is interconnected."—Jane Goodall

How to Use This Book

Community Investigation

Start by discussing the concept of community. Use the *Community Investigation* pages (5–6) to have students research and learn more about the communities they are a part of. Depending on how deeply students delve into their communities, this activity could take days or even weeks. Once students have an established sense of their own communities, it is time to share units about students in other communities and explore what they have accomplished. You may wish to choose a unit based on student interest, or just start at the beginning and do them all!

Informational Text Units

Each six-page unit for informational text learning is set up in the same manner to provide consistency for students. Each unit includes the following components:

- ⌘ **Nonfiction Passage.** Each two-page nonfiction passage features a young person who spots a need in their community and decides to do something about it. These nonfiction texts include a variety of text features to enhance students' understanding and draw attention to important facts. They include subheads, quotes, boldfaced words, sidebars and insets, and vocabulary callouts. Students can read the texts individually or in groups, and they are perfect for repeated readings.

⌘ **Text Questions.** The three pages of text questions each focus on different nonfiction reading skills:

- *Key Ideas and Details* questions ask students to identify what the text says, including the main idea and key details.

- *Craft and Structure* questions focus on the author's craft and organizational patterns, including vocabulary.

- *Integration of Knowledge and Meaning* questions focus on analyzing what the text means, and they also integrate new information with students' own knowledge and experiences.

⌘ **Culminating Unit Activities.** The final page of each unit helps students consolidate the knowledge they have accumulated and consider ways they might put it to use.

- *Group Discussion* questions help students connect the ideas in the text to their own lives and communities. These can be used for either small-group or whole-group discussion.

- *Taking Action* asks students to apply the ideas in the text to a problem in their own communities. These activities help students understand how collaborating in their communities can help them to be part of solutions.

Vocabulary

Some vocabulary words are defined in callouts within the texts. A more extensive vocabulary list is included on pages 7–8, along with a graphic organizer on page 9 that allows students to think about word meanings from multiple angles.

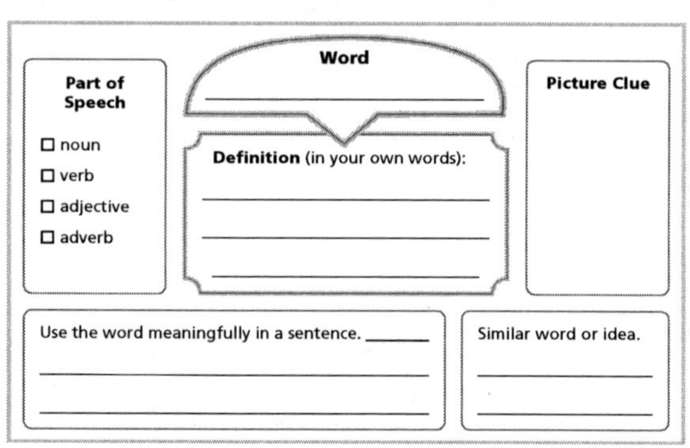

Take Action in Your Community

As a culminating activity, have students use the *Taking Action* activity (pages 10–11) to plan and carry out positive actions in their communities.

- In Part 1, students choose a community and define a problem through research and dialogue with community members.

- In Part 2, they make a plan for action and put it into practice. Students may want to take action individually, in small groups, or even as a project for the entire class.

- In Part 3, students reflect on what they have learned and consider what they might do next.

> **Note to Teacher:** As students plan their projects, consider any safety issues and work with them to create a workable plan.

Community Investigation

Name: ________________________________   **Date:** _________________

Part 1: Defining *Your* Community

> ⇒ *What Is a Community?*
> - a particular area where a group of people live
> - a group of people who live or work close together or have shared interests
> - a feeling of fellowship (belonging) with others as a result of sharing common attitudes, interests, and goals

1. What type of community do you live in?

☐ Urban   ☐ Suburban   ☐ Rural   ☐ Other: _______________

What is the population?____

2. Check off the communities you feel most connected to. Add more if neessary.

☐ Family	☐ Online community	☐ Country
☐ Classroom	☐ Volunteer community	☐ World
☐ School	☐ Neighborhood	☐ ____________
☐ Religious community	☐ Town or city	☐ ____________
☐ Club or scouts	☐ State or region	☐ ____________

3. Which community would you like to focus on? ________________________

4. Who is part of this community? ____________________________________

____

Where do you talk or do things together? _______________________________

What do you have in common? ____

How are you different from one another?_________________________________

5. What does this community do for you?________________________________

____

Name: _________________________________   **Date:** _________________

═══ Part 2: Community Issues and Needs ═══

1. What are some needs you have seen in your community?

____

2. Who offers help in your community? Look for people, places, and organizations that provide information and help to community members. *Example*: In many communities, the public library is an important source of information.

People	Places	Organizations
Who are they?	Where are they?	What are they?
___________	___________	___________
How do they help?	How do they help?	How do they help?
___________	___________	___________
___________	___________	___________
___________	___________	___________

3. Have you seen or been a part of community-service projects?   **Yes   Not yet**

If yes, what worked? ____

____

What didn't work as well? ____

4. If you put together a project to help your community, who could help you?

____

What laws, rules, or customs should you be aware of? ______________

____

____

Vocabulary List

abroad—in a foreign country

accessible—able to be used or to be seen

adopt—to legally take another person's child into your own family and take care of them as your own child

artificial intelligence—the ability of a machine to imitate intelligent human behavior

assembly—a meeting in school for more than one class

buddy bench—a place where kids can sit at recess if they are lonely

caterpillar—a small, long animal with many legs that feeds on the leaves of plants and develops into a butterfly or moth

charity—a group or organization that helps people in need

chemotherapy—using chemicals to treat diseases

chrysalis—a moth or butterfly at the stage of development when it is covered by a hard case, before it becomes an adult insect

coding—writing instructions for a computer to follow

contagious—ability to spread by direct or indirect contact

coordinate—to make different things work together

crisis—a very dangerous or difficult situation

decompose—break down over time into smaller parts

designer—a person who creates a new look or style for an item

disability—a condition that can get in the way of being able to do some things

disposable—meant to be thrown away after use

distribute—to give something out to people

donations—gifts of money, food, clothes, or time to help people

empathy—understanding the feelings of others by putting yourself in their place

epilepsy—a disease of the brain that may cause a person to become unconscious for a short time or to lose control of their movements

evict—to remove people living in a home

exclude—to leave out; to prevent someone or something from entering a place or taking part in an activity

expensive—costing a lot of money

fencing—a sport using a foil or saber

foster—to care for a child while their parents are unable to

fundraising—collecting money for charity

gender bias—when people think boys or girls have to be a certain way

Vocabulary List *(cont.)*

include—invite someone to join you or your group

inclusion—including all people

inclusive—include many different types of people and treat them all fairly and equally

independent—not controlled by others; free

innovate—to do something in a new way

inspire—to give an idea that makes a person take action

interview—a meeting in which someone answers questions about themself for a newspaper article, television show, etc.

inventor—someone who designs or creates something that did not exist before

joystick—a device that can be moved forward, backward, and sideways to control a machine

knitting—using two long needles or a special hoop to connect yarn into joined rows

landfill—a place where lots of trash is buried

litter—trash lying on the ground

medical—relating to the treatment of illness or injury

migrate—to travel to a different place

motto—a short statement meant to inspire

native—living or growing naturally in a region

necessities—items that are needed to live

nectar—a sweet liquid produced by flowers and collected by bees and other insects

obstacles—something that blocks your way so that movement or progress is prevented or made more difficult

organic—grown or raised without artificial chemicals

pitch—a speech that attempts to persuade someone to do something

pledge—a public promise

points of view—ways of thinking and looking at the world

pollution—harmful substances that cause damage to water, the air, or other parts of nature

seizure—a very sudden attack of an illness in which someone becomes unconscious or develops violent movements

senior citizen—an elderly person; a person who is 55 years old or older

snowballed—became important and grew quickly; an idea that spreads

survival—continuing to live

tech—short for technology

volunteer—a helper who does not get paid

wasteful—using something in a careless way and causing some of it to be wasted

Vocabulary Graphic Organizer

Name: ________________________ **Date:** ________________________

Word

Part of Speech

☐ noun

☐ verb

☐ adjective

☐ adverb

Definition (in your own words):

Picture Clue

Use the word meaningfully in a sentence. ________

Similar word or idea:

Word

Part of Speech

☐ noun

☐ verb

☐ adjective

☐ adverb

Definition (in your own words):

Picture Clue

Use the word meaningfully in a sentence. ________

Similar word or idea:

Taking Action

Name: ___________________________________   **Date:** ________________

<hr>

Part 1: The Problem

1. What community will you focus on?

____

2. Who are the members of this community?

____

____

3. What need or problem will you address?

____

4. Research to learn more about the issue.

What is the problem or need? _______________________________________

Who is involved? ____

When and where do things happen? _________________________________

Why is this a problem or a need? ___________________________________

____

5. Listen to others, and talk with them about the issue.

How can you connect with the people involved to find out what would help?

____

What do they say the problem is? __________________________________

____

What do they think would help? ____________________________________

____

Taking Action *(cont.)*

Name: ________________________________   **Date:** ________________

Part 2: Take Action

1. **Define and share** your own ideas.

    What is the specific problem? ____

    ____

    What are your ideas for solutions? ___________________________________

    ____

    How can you share these ideas with those who are affected? ___________

    ____

    How can you share these ideas with those who can make change? ________

    ____

2. **Take action** to address the issue.

    What is your plan of action? ____

    ____

    What is the first step? ____

    ____

Part 3: Reflect

1. **Reflect** on what you have learned about working with your community to accomplish your projects (goals).

    ____

2. What can you do for your community moving forward? __________________

    ____

Christian Bucks

A Great Idea

When Christian Bucks was in first grade, his parents were thinking about moving to another country. They looked at pictures of schools in many places. Christian noticed a brightly colored bench on a playground at one school. He asked his mom to help him find out more about it. They learned that it was called a "buddy bench."

A **buddy bench** is a place where kids can sit if they are lonely at recess. Other kids see them and know how they are feeling. They can go up to someone sitting on a buddy bench and ask them to play. Christian liked the idea of a buddy bench. He wanted to get a buddy bench for his school.

> "A lot of kids, I noticed, were lonely at recess. Like, walking around by themselves with their heads down. They seemed upset. So, I thought the buddy bench would be a great way to give them a friend to play with at recess and to be happy at recess because recess is supposed to be fun."

Christian's Buddy Bench

Christian's family decided not to move away. He stayed in his school and started second grade. Christian asked his principal if they could put a buddy bench on the playground. Mr. Miller, the principal, loved the idea!

Christian and Mr. Miller worked together to pick out and order a bench. They asked students from the local high school to paint the bench in bright, happy colors. Mr. Miller said that they needed to introduce the buddy bench idea to the school board. He asked Christian to give a short talk to explain the buddy bench. The school board thought it was a great idea!

Buddy Bench

Why might kids want to sit on a buddy bench?

- They are new to the school.
- Their friends are absent from school that day.
- They want to make new friends.
- They want to play something different from what they usually play at recess.

Christian Bucks *(cont.)*

Introducing the Buddy Bench

Christian and Mr. Miller needed to introduce the buddy bench to the kids at his school. They made a short video about the buddy bench. In the video, they explained to kids that they could sit on the buddy bench if they were lonely at recess. They told kids that if they saw someone sitting on the buddy bench, they should go talk to them. They should ask if they want to play.

Mr. Miller had a school **assembly** for all the kids. He showed the video. All the kids loved it! They were excited to get out onto the playground to see their new buddy bench.

Spreading the Word

Christian got lots of attention for bringing the buddy bench to his school. The local newspaper took his picture and wrote a story about him. Then, a famous TV show **interviewed** him.

Soon, people all over the country heard about Christian and his buddy bench. Schools called him to ask him about it. He was invited to visit other schools to explain about buddy benches. Christian appeared in newspapers, magazines, children's books, videos, and TV shows. But he didn't want people to talk about him. He wanted them to talk about buddy benches.

Christian's mom helped him start a website where people can find out all about buddy benches. Thousands of schools all across the United States and in other countries now have buddy benches on their playgrounds.

Including People Is Kind

Have you ever felt left out? Maybe you didn't have someone to sit with at lunch. Maybe you don't have someone to play with at recess. Or maybe you were not invited to a party.

Excluding someone means leaving them out. Being excluded hurts people's feelings. Leaving a person out on purpose is a kind of bullying.

One way to be kind to others is to **include** them. If someone asks to play with you, say yes. Be kind and make them feel welcome.

> "My hope is that every school gets a buddy bench and loneliness is cured cause of the buddy bench and new friendships are made."

Name: ___________________________________   **Date:** ____________________

Key Ideas and Details

Directions: Answer the questions below about Christian Bucks. Use complete sentences.

1. What is this text about?

   ____

   ____

2. Name two details that you read about Christian.

   Detail 1: ____

   ____

   Detail 2: ____

   ____

3. The words *include* and *exclude* are opposites. What does it mean to *include* someone?

   ____

   ____

   ____

   What does it mean to *exclude* someone?

   ____

   ____

   ____

Name: _______________________________   **Date:** _________________

Craft and Structure

Directions: Answer the questions below. Use complete sentences.

1. Why do you think the author used a bulleted list to show you why kids might want to sit on a buddy bench?

   ____

   ____

   How does the bulleted list help you understand the text?

   ____

   ____

2. What does the subheading "Spreading the Word" mean?

   ____

   ____

   ____

3. What is a different subheading that the author could have used for the "Spreading the Word" section?

   ____

   ____

   ____

Name: ______________________________ **Date:** ______________

Integration of Knowledge and Meaning

Directions: Answer the questions below. Use complete sentences.

1. Why do you think Christian wanted people to talk about buddy benches and not about him?

   ____

   ____

2. Do you agree with the author that, "Being excluded hurts people's feelings"?

   Yes   **No**

   Why or why not? ______________________________________

   ____

3. Write about a time when you included someone or a time when someone included you.

   ____

   ____

   How did it make you feel?

   ____

   ____

Name: ___________________________   **Date:** ___________________

Group Discussion

Brainstorming: Have you ever felt excluded?

- ✿ Why do you think you felt that way?
- ✿ How can you tell if someone doesn't feel included?
- ✿ What could you do to help them feel more welcome?

Taking Action

Directions: Think of a situation in which someone might not feel included. List some things you could do to help them and some things you should not do.

Things I can say	Things I should NOT say

Things I can do	Things I should NOT do

Aiden Wang

Beautiful Butterflies

When he was in first grade, Aiden Wang's class hatched Monarch butterflies. The class watched small caterpillars hatch from eggs. The caterpillars ate leaves. They grew and grew. Then, the caterpillars hung upside down. They formed hard shells around their bodies. The shell is called a **chrysalis**. The class waited for the hard shells to crack open. When they did, the kids were amazed! The caterpillars were gone. Beautiful orange and black butterflies came out. Aiden loved watching the butterflies flutter off when they were let go.

Aiden wanted to know more about the butterflies. He did some research. He learned that Monarch caterpillars eat the leaves of milkweed plants. He also found out that Monarch butterflies are in trouble. In the United States, **native** milkweed plants are dying from weed killer. There isn't enough milkweed to feed the caterpillars. Aiden decided he wanted to help.

Helping the Monarchs

Aiden got some milkweed seeds. He planted them in pots and put them outside. He watered the plants and they grew. For the first two years, Aiden did not find any butterfly eggs on his milkweed plants. But he kept caring for the plants. He didn't give up. The third year, he finally found some Monarch eggs. He was ready to help the butterflies grow. Here is what he did:

- First, he clipped off the section of the leaf where the **eggs** were. He put the eggs inside in a plastic box. This helped the eggs stay safe from hard rain and other insects.

- Then, when the **caterpillars** hatched, Aiden gave them lots of milkweed leaves to eat. They grew quickly!

- He waited until each caterpillar formed a **chrysalis**. He put the chrysalises into a net cage.

- He waited some more. The hard shells cracked open. Wet **butterflies** came out. They needed about an hour for their wings to dry. Then, they could fly.

Aiden Wang *(cont.)*

Butterflies Need Nectar

Butterflies get their food from flowers. They sip **nectar** from flowers. Aiden took his 25 butterflies to an **organic** farm. The farmer didn't use any weed killers. Aiden's butterflies would be safe.

Butterflies Need Our Help

Monarch butterflies **migrate** every year. They fly from a cold place to a warm place. They start in the northern United States and Canada. They travel to California and Mexico. They fly over 2,000 miles.

Over one million Monarchs made the trip 10 years ago. Now, the numbers are much smaller. Monarch butterflies need healthy milkweed plants to lay their eggs on. Monarch caterpillars need to eat milkweed leaves. They cannot grow without them. Aiden knows his work is helping. He explains:

> "The **survival** rate for Monarch butterfly eggs in the wild is 5 to 10 percent. When raised indoors, their survival rate shoots up to 95 percent."

He keeps growing milkweed plants. Every year, he saves more and more caterpillars. Almost all of his butterflies live. Aiden let over 400 Monarch butterflies go last year. He helped 400 caterpillars change into butterflies!

Aiden wants people to plant milkweed and other flowering plants for the butterflies.

Help Native Species

Many wild plants and animals need our help. They are dying because of problems caused by people. How can we help? We need to do our part to help stop climate change, **pollution**, and habitat loss.

- **Clean Up:** Pick up your trash. Animals can get caught in things like six-pack rings. They eat small bits of plastic that make them sick. Always make sure you put your trash where it won't end up on the ground or in the water.

- **Keep It Natural:** Many people use chemicals to kill pests and to grow plants quickly. Don't use chemicals near plants or animals.

- **Plant Native Plants:** Native plants are plants that have always grown where you live. They did not come from far away. Planting native plants helps provide food and shelter for native animals.

Name: _______________________________________   **Date:** _______________________

Key Ideas and Details

Directions: Answer the questions below about Aiden Wang. Use complete sentences.

1. Who or what is this text mainly about? Name two details that tell you about the main idea.

Detail 1: ____

____

Detail 2: ____

____

2. How does Aiden Wang help Monarch butterflies?

____

____

3. Draw the stages of the Monarch butterfly life cycle.

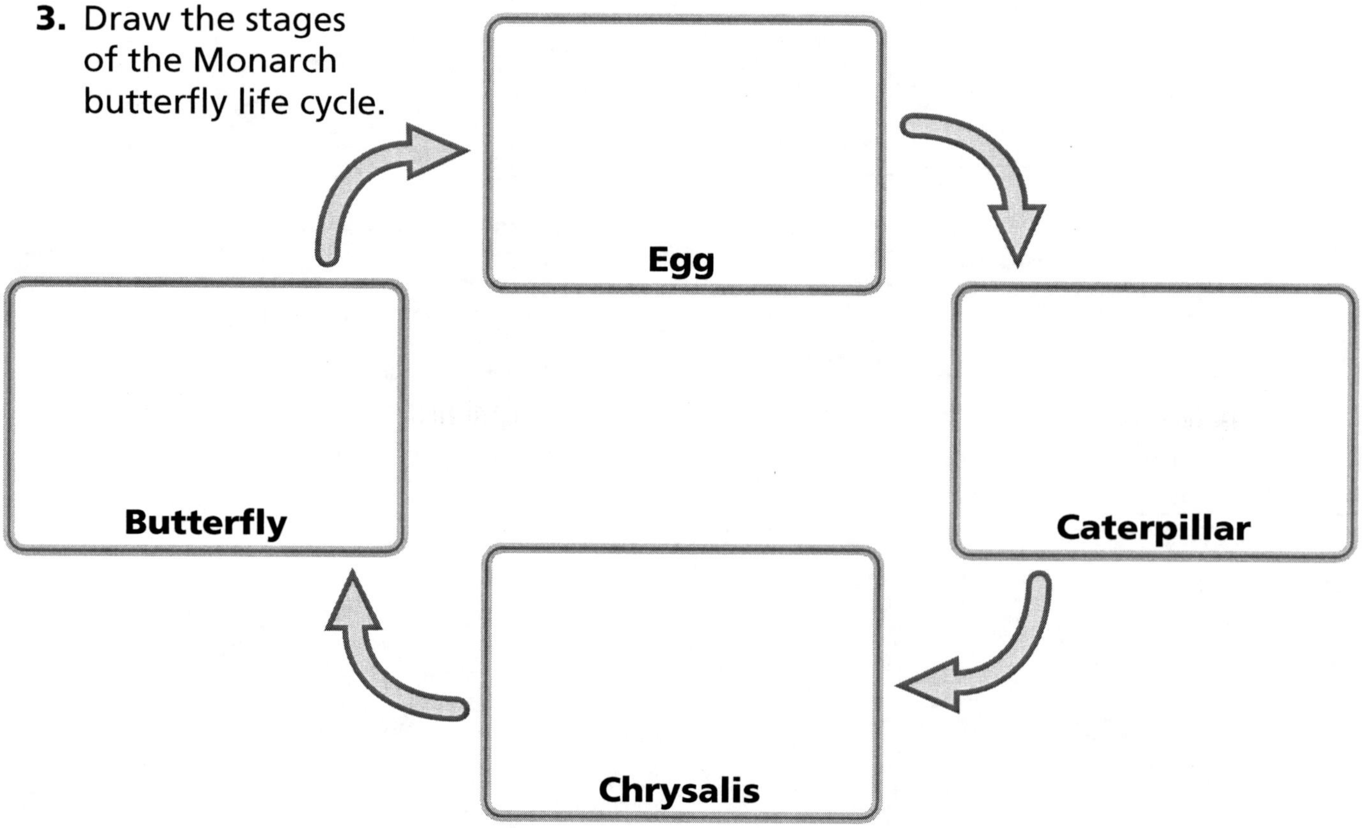

Egg

Caterpillar

Chrysalis

Butterfly

Name: ___________________________________   **Date:** _________________

Craft and Structure

Directions: Answer the questions below. Use complete sentences.

1. What does *migrate* mean? Use the other words and sentences in the text to help you understand it.

____

____

2. Why do you think the author included the sidebar about helping *native* species?

____

____

3. Choose one word from the text that you think is important to understanding Aiden's story. Define the word, and explain its importance to the story.

Word: ____

Definition: ____

____

____

Importance to the story: _______________________________________

____

____

____

Name: _________________________________ **Date:** _______________

Integration of Knowledge and Meaning

Directions: Answer the questions below. Use complete sentences.

1. The text says, "Aiden wants people to plant milkweed and other flowering plants for the butterflies." How would this help the butterflies?

   ____

   ____

   ____

2. Why do you think it is important to protect native plants and animals?

   ____

   ____

   ____

3. Name two animals and two plants that are *native* to your area.

   Animals _____________________________   _____________________________

   Plants _____________________________   _____________________________

4. Name a plant and an animal that are *not native* to your area.

   Animal _____________________________   **Plant** _____________________________

Name: ___________________________   **Date:** _______________

Group Discussion

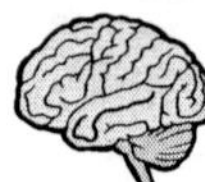 **Brainstorming:** Think about the animals that live near your home.

- ⌘ What native animals live near you?
- ⌘ What problems do they face?
- ⌘ What do they need?
- ⌘ How could you find out more?

=== **Taking Action** ===

Directions: Use this graphic organizer to do research about an animal.

What is the problem?

____

____

____

____

What is being done?

____

____

____

Draw an animal to help.

What can I do to help?

____

____

____

Who might help me?

____

____

Garrett Lowry

Giving to Others

Garrett Lowry has always enjoyed helping others. When he was just seven years old, he donated all his birthday toys to a local **charity**. He wanted to give toys to kids who had none.

At the age of ten, he participated in a giving project at school. All of the kids had to do something to help others. Garrett's grandmother had taught him to knit when he was young. It helped him keep calm and learn to focus. Garrett decided to knit hats for kids who have cancer. They get **chemotherapy** to make them better. Many people who get chemotherapy lose their hair. The knit hats keep them warm and cozy.

Garrett's goal was to knit and donate ten hats. With help from his mother and grandmother, he kept going. He knitted 50 hats! He donated them to a local children's hospital. But he didn't stop there. Garrett kept on **knitting**. He has now donated over 100 hats to cancer patients.

Personal Experience

Why does Garrett want to help cancer patients? It is because of his personal experiences.

- ⌘ His grandfather died from cancer.
- ⌘ He has a younger friend who is fighting cancer. Garrett says she is a hero for fighting through pain and fear.
- ⌘ His cat died from cancer.
- ⌘ He hopes that his **donations** will help cancer patients feel just a little bit better. He wants them to know that someone cares about them.

"Going through that kind of thing might scare people, and I just want to make something that can make them more comfortable while they are in the hospital."

Garrett Lowry *(cont.)*

What Will They Think?

Garrett loves sports. He runs track and plays basketball, football, and baseball. His baseball team calls him "Bam Bam" because he is such a powerful hitter. He worried what his teammates would think when they found out he also liked to knit.

But Garrett thinks it is important to help others. He spread his message of kindness to his baseball team. He helped them donate gifts to families in need.

Garrett continues to give to others. He plans to **volunteer** at the children's hospital when he is old enough.

volunteer—a helper who does not get paid

Men Who Knit

What do you think of when you hear the word *knitting*? Many people think of their grandmother making scarves and sweaters. But knitting is not just for women!

Gender bias is when people think boys or girls have to be a certain way. But boys can enjoy knitting just as much as girls like playing baseball. Men enjoy knitting for many different reasons. It is an activity that helps people feel calm. It allows them to be creative. And they enjoy making gifts for others.

Name: ___________________________________ **Date:** _________________

Key Ideas and Details

Directions: Answer the questions below about Garrett Lowry. Use complete sentences.

1. What is this text about?

____

____

____

2. How did Garrett learn to knit?

____

____

____

3. Why did Garrett want to knit hats?

____

____

____

4. What is one piece of text evidence that tells you about how Garrett feels?

____

____

____

Name: _________________________________ **Date:** ______________

Craft and Structure

Directions: Answer the questions below. Use complete sentences.

1. What does the word *charity* mean?

____

____

____

2. Why does the author use a bulleted list in the "Personal Experiences" section?

____

____

____

3. Why do you think the author included the "Men Who Knit" sidebar?

____

____

____

4. What does the quote from Garrett tell you about him?

____

____

____

Name: _________________________________ **Date:** _______________

Integration of Knowledge & Meaning

Directions: Answer the questions below. Use complete sentences.

1. How do the illustrations help you understand the text?

   ____

   ____

   ____

   ____

2. Why do you think Garrett was worried about what his baseball teammates might think about his knitting?

   ____

   ____

   ____

   ____

3. Why do you think Garrett enjoys giving to others?

   ____

   ____

   ____

   ____

Name: _______________________________   **Date:** _______________________

Group Discussion

Brainstorming: Garrett knits hats to help cancer patients feel a bit better.

- ⌘ Who else might need support and cheering up?
- ⌘ What could you do for them?

Taking Action

Garrett didn't let *gender bias* stop him from doing something he enjoyed.

Directions: What is something you like to do that people might not expect? How could you use that skill or activity to help others? Make a plan.

My skill or activity:

____

____

Two ways I can use it to help others:

A'Layah Robinson

Foster Home to Forever Home

A'Layah Robinson has always wanted to help others. When she was four, she saved all her birthday and Christmas money. She wanted to buy a toy car she could ride in. Then, a tornado hit the town where she lives. The tornado caused a lot of damage. A'Layah decided to give all her money to a family that had lost everything.

A'Layah knew what it was like to lose everything. She had been a **foster** kid. Her own parents could not take care of her. She and her brother moved from house to house and lived with different people. These people took care of them. When she met her new mom, A'Layah only owned a few items. Her little brother had nothing.

> "When my brother was a little baby, he only came home with a diaper he was wearing and a shirt that was too small for him and some little shoes. So I went in my brand new room, and I got a block and a stuffed animal."

A'Layah and her brother were soon **adopted**. They would not have to move around in foster homes anymore. They found their forever home with their new mom.

Foster Kids

Foster kids are not able to live with their birth families. Their own parents are not able to take care of them. Many times, foster kids have to leave their homes quickly. They don't get to take their things with them. They go to live in someone else's home for a while. This home is called a foster home. They live there until they can go back home or be adopted.

Many foster kids do not have things of their own. They don't have toys. Sometimes, they only have the clothes they are wearing. Foster families try to help them and buy them what they need. But sometimes, foster families don't have much extra money to help.

Many foster kids spend a short time in foster care. Some have to move to a few different foster homes. Some foster kids go back to their parents. Others are adopted by new families.

A'Layah Robinson *(cont.)*

A Lemonade Stand of Her Own

One day when A'Layah was only five years old, she and her mom saw some teenagers with a lemonade stand. A'Layah was curious. She wanted to know what the kids were doing. She found out that the kids were raising money. They wanted to help a friend buy clothes for a very special birthday. A'Layah liked the idea of helping others. She was **inspired**. She wanted to have her own lemonade stand. She wanted to raise money to help foster kids!

> ➠ **inspire**—to give an idea that makes a person take action

A'Layah's family helped her set up a lemonade stand. Her mom bought lemons and sugar to make the lemonade. Her grandparents helped, too. They bought cups and ice for the stand. Their first lemonade stand earned $132.

Giving Back

A'Layah decided to use the money from the lemonade stand to make gift bags for foster kids. She wanted them to feel better. She knew some things that they could use. She decided what to put in each bright yellow bag.

- She remembered that her little brother had no toys when he first came home. A'Layah put a brand new toy in every gift bag.

- She remembered when she had to clean her teeth with a rag. She put in a toothbrush and toothpaste.

- She remembered what it was like to sleep outside because one of her foster families was **evicted** from their home. She put blankets in her gift bags to keep kids warm.

> ➠ **evict**—to remove people living in a home

A'Layah and her family continued to raise money. A'Layah's goal is to buy a toy for every foster kid in the world!

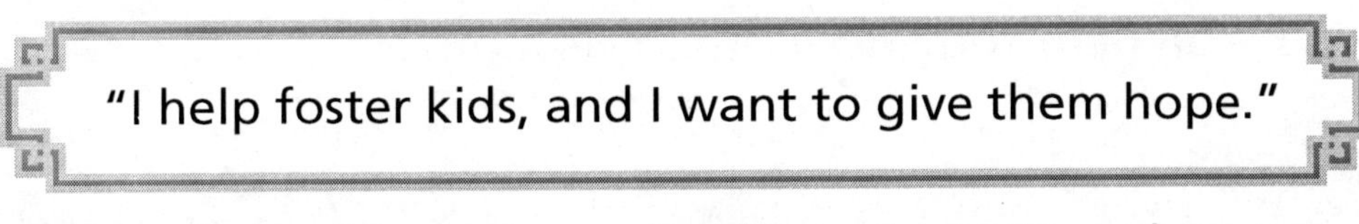
"I help foster kids, and I want to give them hope."

Her mom helped her start a **charity** called "A'Layah's Lemonade for Love." People donate money to the charity. That money helps give gift bags to foster kids. A'Layah and her family and friends put the bags together. So far, A'Layah's charity has packed gift bags for more than 1,000 kids!

Name: _________________________________   **Date:** _________________

Key Ideas and Details

Directions: Answer the questions below about A'Layah Robinson. Use complete sentences.

1. What is the main idea of this text?

____

____

____

____

2. What details most helped you understand the main idea?

In the text it says ____

____

____

____

3. Why did A'Layah want to help foster kids?

____

____

____

What details in the text can help you answer this question?

____

____

Name: _______________________________   **Date:** _______________

Craft and Structure

Directions: Answer the questions below. Use complete sentences.

1. What does *adopted* mean? How do the words around it help you understand what it means?

____

____

____

2. Why do you think the author included the inset about foster kids?

____

____

____

3. Choose two words or phrases the author used and explain how they helped you understand the text better.

Word 1: _______________________________

____

____

____

Word 2: _______________________________

____

____

____

Name: ___________________________________   **Date:** _______________________

Integration of Knowledge and Meaning

Directions: Answer the questions below. Use complete sentences.

1. Explain how A'Layah used an experience in her life to inspire her to help others.

   ____

   ____

   ____

   ____

2. What experiences have you had that you could use as inspiration for making a difference?

   ____

   ____

   ____

   ____

3. What person or group would you like to raise money for?

   ____

   ____

   Why? ____

   ____

   ____

Name: ______________________________   **Date:** ___________________

Group Discussion

Brainstorming: A'Layah Robinson faced hard times in her life. She used these experiences to help others.

⌘ What other experiences might people use to inspire them?

⌘ How can you turn a difficulty into something positive?

Taking Action

A'Layah Robinson wanted to help foster kids because she had been a foster kid. She had the same problems they have.

Directions: Think of a problem you have faced and how you could use that experience to help others.

What is a problem you have faced that other kids might also have faced?

____

____

____

How could you find out if others have the same problem?

____

____

____

What kind of group could you create to help face the problem?

____

____

____

Hailey Scheinman

◄— Sisters and Best Friends —►

Hailey and Olivia are twins. Olivia is called "Livy." Hailey is healthy but Livy was born with **medical** challenges. She cannot speak or sit up by herself. Her body moves in ways she cannot control. She needs help every day.

> ⇒ **medical**—relating to the treatment of an illness or an injury

Livy has to take many different medicines. She needs special treatments to help her. She also needs surgeries. Someone needs to take care of her all day.

Hailey and Livy may be different but they are very close. Hailey brushes Livy's hair and helps feed her. Livy loves it when Hailey reads books to her. Livy smiles her beautiful smile when Hailey is around.

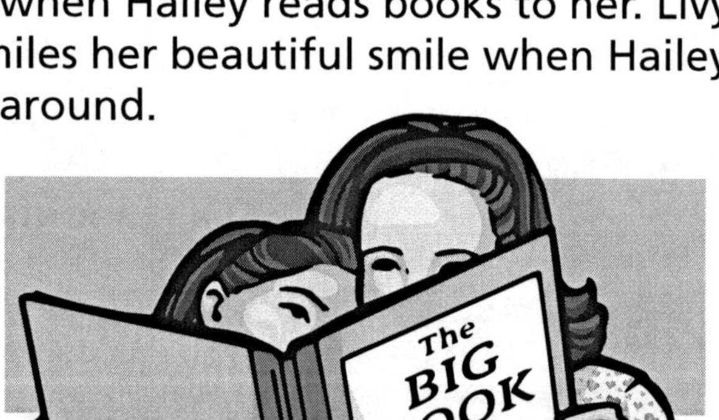

Epilepsy

One of Livy's medical challenges is called **epilepsy**. Many people have epilepsy.

People who have epilepsy have **seizures**. A seizure is when the brain sends out too many signals for a short time.

People who have seizures can shake all over or fall down. Some people just stare into space when it happens. It depends on the kind of seizure. It can be scary for the person having the seizure. It can also be scary for the people around them.

People with epilepsy cannot control the seizures. They cannot make them stop. Many people don't even know when they have one. Some people only have a seizure once in a while. Other people have seizures all the time. Livy is like that. Livy has many seizures every day.

Epilepsy is not **contagious**. You can't catch it from anyone. There is no reason to be afraid. It is important to learn about it.

> "Her smile is so pure and she's always happy. Livy is my best friend in the whole world. Whenever I'm sad about something, I just go find Livy and give her a hug and she makes me feel better. More than anything, Livy gives people hope."

Hailey Scheinman *(cont.)*

Hailey Helps Her Family

One time, Hailey heard her parents talking. They said that Livy's medical care was getting **expensive**. They needed more money. There were a lot of bills.

> ➠ **expensive**—costing a lot of money

Hailey wanted to help. She decided to help raise money. It would help pay for Livy's medical care. What could she do? She was in kindergarten!

- She made beaded bracelets and painted pictures to sell.

- Her family helped her make an online store so she could sell her art. It worked!

- Hailey also started a lemonade stand called "Lemonade for Livy."

Livy's Hope

Hailey's family decided to put all their **fundraising** ideas together. They started a charity. They call their charity "Livy's Hope." All the money they raise goes to help kids with challenges like Livy. Their family **motto** is, "Don't give up. Give back!"

Hailey is very busy with school and her activities. She spends time with her sister. Hailey also helps others. She and her family now work with the Epilepsy Foundation. They started a program called Kids Crew. Hailey is a leader in the Kids Crew. She gives talks to different groups and schools. The goal is to help kids learn more about epilepsy from other kids.

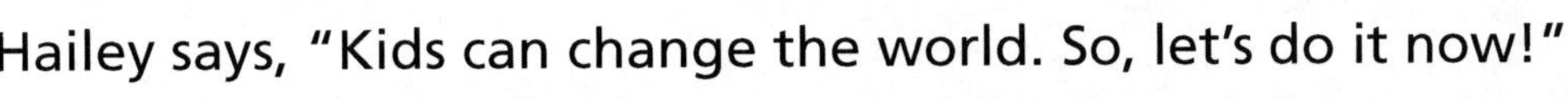

Now, there are many Kids Crews all over the United States. Members of Kids Crew meet every month. They do many different things to help give back.

- They make friends with kids who have epilepsy.

- They plan events to raise money to help kids with epilepsy.

- They teach others how to be kind and **inclusive**. That means they try not to leave anyone out because of differences.

> Hailey says, "Kids can change the world. So, let's do it now!"

Name: ___________________________________ **Date:** ___________________

Key Ideas and Details

Directions: Answer the questions below about Hailey Scheinman. Use complete sentences.

1. What are two details that tell you about Hailey?

   Detail 1: ____

   ____

   Detail 2: ____

   ____

2. What is *epilepsy*?

   ____

   ____

   ____

   Why is epilepsy treatment *expensive*?

   ____

   ____

3. If you were going to write a new title for this text, what would it be and why?

   Title: ____

   Why? ____

   ____

Name: _______________________________   **Date:** _______________

Craft and Structure

Directions: Answer the questions below. Use complete sentences.

1. What does *fundraising* mean? How do the words around it help you understand what it means?

____

____

2. Why do you think the author included the first quote from Hailey? What does it tell you about her?

____

____

3. The *motto* for Livy's Hope is "Don't give up. Give back!" What is a motto?

____

What does this motto mean?

____

____

4. Why do you think the author uses bulleted lists in the passage?

____

____

Do you think bulleted lists are helpful?   **Yes**   **No**

Why? ____

____

Name: _________________________________   **Date:** _______________

Integration of Knowledge and Meaning

Directions: Answer the questions below. Use complete sentences.

1. Why did Hailey want to sell her paintings and jewelry?

____

____

2. Have you ever done any fundraising?   **Yes**   **No**

If yes, what was the money for? _______________________________

If you have not done it before, who or what would you like to raise money for?

____

Why? ____

____

3. What more would you like to know about Hailey and Livy Scheinman?

____

____

Why? ____

____

____

Name: _________________________________ **Date:** _______________

Group Discussion

 **Brainstorming:** Hailey uses her talents and interests to help others. She creates paintings and jewelry and sells them to raise money.

⌘ What talents and interests do you have?

⌘ How could you use them to help others? For example, soccer teams could raise money for each goal they score. Kids who sing could perform at homes for elderly patients to cheer them up.

Taking Action

Directions: Think of a talent or interest you or your class could use to help your community. Fill out the graphic organizer to plan your sharing.

What can you share?

____

____

____

Who can you share it with?

____

____

____

When would you share?

____

____

____

Where would you share?

____

____

____

Why would you share?

____

____

____

Hana Fatima

A Helping Hand

Hana Fatima and her father were at the grocery store. It was during the Covid-19 pandemic. The lines were long. They had to wait an hour to shop. People were buying everything! The shelves were getting empty. Hana and her dad just wanted to get their groceries and hurry home.

As they were checking out, Hana saw an older lady. She was having trouble carrying all her grocery bags. Hana pointed the woman out to her father. She wanted to help her. They helped carry the lady's bags to her car. Hana could tell that the lady felt better. Helping made Hana feel good!

> "It made me think of my grandparents. She got really happy."

When they got home, Hana remembered there were some **senior citizens** on her street who might also need help. Hana and her dad wrote their phone number on cards. They gave the cards to their neighbors who might need help. They told them to call if they needed any help. When Hana's family went to the store, they would get things for their neighbors. They would deliver the groceries for free.

➡ **senior citizen**—an elderly person; someone who is 55 years old or older

More Helping Hands

Hana's dad asked a few friends if they wanted to help. Those friends asked more friends. Hana's idea to help her neighbors **snowballed**. Hana's dad created a group on social media. The group connected with more people who wanted to help. They called their group The Good Neighbour* Project. Pretty soon, there were hundreds of people helping their neighbors! Another word for these helpers is **volunteers**. Volunteers are helpers who do not want to get paid.

➡ **snowballed**—became important and grew quickly; an idea that spreads

*The Good Neighbour Project started in Canada. There, they use a different spelling for "neighbor" than in the United States. They add a "u," just like they do in England.

Hana Fatima *(cont.)*

The Good Neighbour Project

The Good Neighbour Project kept growing. It had more than 6,000 members. They were all helping their neighbors. They took food to people who needed to stay at home. They also dropped off medicine and other supplies. They had a list of people who needed help to stay safe:

- senior citizens
- disabled persons
- people in quarantine
- women who were pregnant
- single parents who needed to stay home with children
- health care workers who did not have time to shop because they were working

Making the Project Work

The project was a good idea, and it grew fast. They needed a way to **coordinate** the deliveries. Here is how the volunteers made it work:

Step 1—Call
A person who needs to stay at home calls a phone number.

Step 2—Connect
The volunteer who answers connects that person with a volunteer in their neighborhood.

Step 3—Pick up
Volunteers pick up groceries, medicine, or other items from stores.

Step 4—Deliver
Volunteers deliver what is needed to the homes of people who called for help.
Some volunteers help food banks deliver free food.
Some volunteers help deliver hot meals during cold weather.

The Good Neighbour Project has coordinated more than 9,000 deliveries. A few volunteers delivered over 200 times!

"When I saw the elderly person, I thought that was my opportunity to go and help somebody… Because whenever you get a chance to be helpful and kind, just go and do it without thinking about it. Everybody should do that. You see an opportunity? Somebody needs help? Just go and do it."

Name: _________________________________   **Date:** ___________________

Key Ideas and Details

Directions: Answer the questions below about Hana Fatima. Use complete sentences.

1. What is the main idea of this text?

____

____

2. What are two details that helped you understand the main idea?

Detail 1: ____

____

Detail 2: ____

____

3. How can someone get help from The Good Neighbour Project? Explain the steps.

Step 1: ____

____

Step 2: ____

____

Step 3: ____

____

Step 4: ____

____

Name: _________________________________   **Date:** _________________

Craft and Structure

Directions: Answer the questions below. Use complete sentences.

1. What does *coordinate* mean? How do the words around it help you understand what it means?

   ____

   ____

   ____

2. Why do you think the author included a bulleted list? How does it help you understand the information?

   ____

   ____

   ____

3. Why do you think the author included the quote from Hana at the end of the text?

   ____

   ____

   What does the quote at the end tell you about Hana?

   ____

   ____

   ____

Name: ________________________________   **Date:** __________________

Integration of Knowledge and Meaning

Directions: Answer the questions below. Use complete sentences.

1. How did Hana feel when she and her father helped the lady carry her groceries to her car?

   ____

   ____

2. Have you ever helped someone? How did it make you feel?

   ____

   ____

   ____

   If you haven't helped someone, would you like to? Why?

   ____

   ____

   ____

3. Why do you think so many people volunteered to help their neighbors?

   ____

   ____

   ____

Name: ________________________   **Date:** ________________

Group Discussion

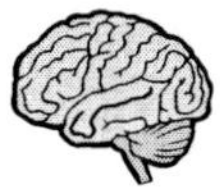

Brainstorming: Hana saw the lady struggling with her groceries. She imagined how she would feel in the same situation. That helped her understand how the woman felt. Understanding the feelings of others by putting yourself in their place is called **empathy**.

- ⌘ Talk about a time when you empathized with someone.
- ⌘ How did you know what they were feeling?
- ⌘ Did you do anything about it? Why or why not?

Taking Action

Think of a problem someone you know has. Talk to the person about it.

Directions: Use the Empathy Map below to record evidence about how they feel. Then, use this information to think of a way to help them.

Problem: ____

Who has this problem? ____

What they say	**What they do**
What they think	**What they feel**

Empathy Map

What did you learn about how this person feels? ____________________

____

What did you learn about the problem? ____________________

____

What can you do to help? ____________________

____

Jane Velkovski

Jane Loves Football

Jane lives in Macedonia. It is a country in Europe. Soccer is called football there. It is a hugely popular sport. Eleven-year-old Jane Velkovski loves football!

Jane is the captain of his football team. He also plays goalie. He leads the team. He calls out directions to the other players. The whole team loves and respects Captain Jane. Jane's eyes light up whenever he talks about his favorite sport.

Names

Jane is pronounced *Yah-nay* in Macedonia.

> "Football is everything in my life," Jane explains. "I play it in video games, I play it in our garden, and I play it at school. I play football everywhere."

Doing Things His Own Way

Playing football is a little bit different for Jane than for his teammates. Jane has a disease that affects his muscles. This means he cannot walk. He uses an electric wheelchair. He drives it with a **joystick** that looks like a football.

Jane says he can do everything that everyone else can. He just does some things in a different way. He studies hard in school. His favorite subject is math. He has lots of friends. He loves to play with his dog, Bella. He plays his favorite sport as much as he can.

Everyone Is Equal

Jane's parents help him to do the things he wants. Sometimes, there are **obstacles** in his way. For example, a building might have stairs but no ramp. Then, he can't get into the building. It is not **accessible**. Jane's parents help him get around these obstacles. If there is anything he can't do, his mother, his father, or his brother help him out.

Jane tries to do things himself. He wants to be **independent**. He believes that the world should be accessible to everyone.

Jane Velkovski *(cont.)*

Jane wants all kids to be able to play sports. He speaks out to share his message. He says that everyone should be treated the same. Everyone should have respect. He works with professional football players to spread his ideas. It is a message of **inclusion**.

> ➠ **inclusion**—including all people

We should treat all people with respect and kindness. We should be aware that there are many ways to do things. Kids with disabilities should be able to go to school. They should be able to play with their friends and play sports. Everyone should be included as much as possible.

> "I want to tell the whole world that everyone is equal and that people with disabilities can do the same things everyone else can. And even if they can't, that doesn't mean they can't enjoy their lives."

About Disability

More than one billion people in the world have a **disability**. A disability is something that can get in the way of being able to do some things. Some disabilities you can see and some you can't.

There are many different kinds of disabilities:

- Some you are born with. Others can happen after an injury or sickness.
- Some affect the body. Others affect the way a person thinks.
- Some last a short time, like when you break an arm or leg. Others will always be a part of a person's life.

There are many ways to work with disabilities to do things. Here are some examples:

- Hearing aids or special computers make it easier for people to hear, talk, or write.
- Wheelchairs, special bikes, canes, and crutches help people move around.

Name: ____   **Date:** ______________________

Key Ideas and Details

Directions: Answer the questions below about Jane Velkovski. Use complete sentences.

1. Who and what is this text mainly about?

   ____

   ____

   ____

   Think of a new title for this text. _____________________________________

   ____

2. How does Jane Velkovski help others?

   ____

   ____

   ____

3. Be the teacher! Write two questions that a teacher might ask about this text.

   Question 1: ____

   ____

   Question 2: ____

   ____

Name: _______________________________ **Date:** _______________

Craft and Structure

Directions: Answer the questions below. Use complete sentences.

1. What does *accessible* mean? How do the words and sentences in the text help you understand what it means?

   ____

   ____

   ____

2. Why do you think the author included the quotes from Jane Velkovski?

   ____

   ____

   ____

3. How does the inset "About Disability" help you understand the rest of the text?

   ____

   ____

   ____

Name: ___________________________________ **Date:** _______________________

Integration of Knowledge and Meaning

Directions: Answer the questions below. Use complete sentences.

1. The text says that sometimes there are *obstacles* in Jane's way. What does this mean?

   ____

   ____

   What are some obstacles that get in your way?

   ____

   ____

2. Jane says that everyone should be treated with respect. Give two examples of treating someone with respect.

   Example 1: ____

   ____

   Example 2: ____

   ____

3. How do you think working with professional football (soccer) players helps Jane spread his message?

   ____

   ____

   ____

Name: _________________________________   **Date:** _________________

Group Discussion

Brainstorming: Jane Velkovski works to make sure everyone is included. What does the word *included* mean to you?

- ⌘ Where and when do you feel included?
- ⌘ In what situations might you not feel that way?
- ⌘ When and where might others not feel included?
- ⌘ How could you help someone feel more included?

Taking Action

Directions: Plan to help your school community include everyone. Think about the thoughts, words, and actions people in your school might use that either exclude (leave out) or include others. Record your ideas in this chart:

	Exclude	Include
Thoughts		
Words		
Actions		

Who might be excluded in your school community? _________________________

____

How might you help your school community become more inclusive? __________

____

Jahkil Naeem Jackson

Inspired to Help

Jahkil Naeem Jackson went with his family to downtown Chicago. He remembers that cold winter day well. His auntie had made a huge batch of chili. It was for people living on the streets. Jahkil and his cousins handed out warm bowls of chili.

Jahkil was only five years old, but he knew that the people were hurting. He wondered why they were hungry. He saw them sleeping outside in the cold. He wanted to help. He asked his parents if they could buy homes for everyone.

For three years, Jahkil thought about how he could help. He brainstormed ideas with his parents. He talked to them about the things that his family had. He knew people without homes did not always have these things.

Many people take for granted things like toothpaste, toothbrushes, socks, and tissues. People who live on the streets can't always get these things. Jahkil decided to fill bags with supplies to hand out to people.

> "Almost every time I see a man in the street, a family in a shelter, a kid in a line waiting for food, I think to myself, that could be me, that could be us. Thinking about folks that way makes it really personal and it's impossible NOT to help."

Blessing Bags

Jahkil decided to fill the bags with basic items. He called them "blessing bags" because he felt that he had been blessed. He had a home and a family. He planned to **distribute** the bags to those who needed them. He wanted to share his blessings with those who were not as lucky.

First, Jahkil asked friends and family to meet him at a local game arcade. He asked them to bring items to put in the blessing bags. He collected wipes, deodorant, granola bars, first-aid items, hand sanitizer, and other **necessities**. Then, Jahkil's family treated everyone to pizza and games. They filled 88 blessing bags that day! Jahkil and his family delivered those bags to people living on the streets in Chicago.

> ⇒ **necessities**—items that are needed to live

Jahkil Naeem Jackson *(cont.)*

Spreading the Word

> "I don't have the words to describe how it felt to look someone in the eye, give them blessings, and wish them well."

Over time, Jahkil's project grew. His parents helped him create a website. They collected **donations** to buy items for more blessing bags. Jahkil appeared on TV and in newspapers. He asked people to help one another. More donations came in. Schools invited him to speak about his project. Each time he spoke at a school, the students donated items for blessing bags.

➠ **donations**—gifts of money, food, clothes, or time to help people

Today, Jahkil's blessing bags have been distributed in many cities across America. He has also provided blessing bags for:

- orphans in Africa
- volcano victims in Guatemala
- hurricane survivors in the Caribbean islands

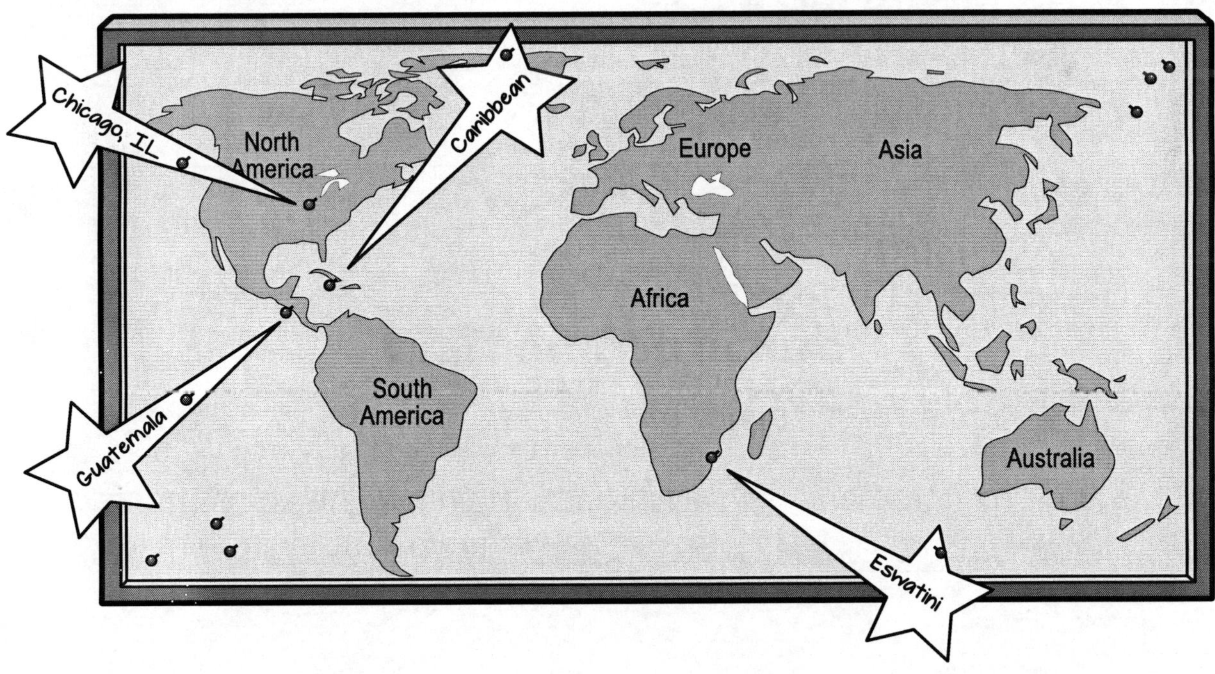

Don't Wait to Be Great!

Jahkil's work has helped over 50,000 people. He speaks to young people all over the United States. He tells his story. He asks them to look around and see who is in need. He knows that they don't have to wait until they are adults to start helping others. He inspires them with his motto, "Don't wait to be great!"

Name: _________________________________   Date: ________________

Key Ideas and Details

Directions: Answer the questions below about Jahkil Naeem Jackson. Use complete sentences.

1. What is the main idea of this text?

   ____

   ____

   ____

2. What inspired Jahkil to help people who live on the streets?

   ____

   ____

3. Who helped Jahkil with his project?

   ____

   ____

   What are two ways they helped him?

   ____

   ____

   ____

Name: _______________________________ **Date:** _______________

Craft and Structure

Directions: Answer the questions below. Use complete sentences.

1. What does *distribute* mean? Use context clues to help you understand this word.

   ____

   ____

2. Why do you think the author began the text with the story of Jahkil's family handing out chili?

   ____

   ____

3. What does the phrase "take for granted" mean?

   ____

   ____

4. What did the map show you?

   ____

   ____

Name: _________________________________   **Date:** _________________

Integration of Knowledge and Meaning

Directions: Answer the questions below. Use complete sentences.

1. Jahkil feels that having a home and a family who loves him are blessings. Some people call this good fortune. What do you think are your blessings?

   ____

   ____

   ____

2. Why do you think Jahkil chose to give people necessities like socks and soap instead of food and blankets?

   ____

   ____

3. If you were filling a blessing bag, what items would you put in it? Why?

   ____

   ____

   ____

   ____

Name: ___________________________________   **Date:** _________________

Group Discussion

Brainstorming: Think about the problems in your community.

⌘ What problems do you know about?   ⌘ How do you know about the problems?   ⌘ How could you find out more?

=========== **Taking Action** ===========

Think about problems you have noticed in your community. Is there trash on the street? Do younger kids need help with homework? Choose a problem and make a plan to help.

Directions: Use this graphic organizer to do research and plan a project.

What is the problem? ___________________________________

____

What is already being done? ___________________________

____

What can I do to help? _________________________________

____

What challenges might I face?	**What kinds of help might I need?**	**Who might be able to help?**

Samaira Mehta

Coding Is Fun

When Samaira Mehta was little, her dad showed her how to code. She learned to write instructions for a computer to follow. He helped her code some simple games. Samaira loved it. She thought it was like magic!

Samaira tried to share her love of **coding** with her friends. But they thought it was too hard or too boring. Samaira wondered why she loved coding but her friends did not. She decided to do something to help her friends see how fun coding can be.

"Learning is so much easier when it is fun!"

CoderBunnyz

Samaira started working on a board game to teach coding skills when she was six years old! She combined two things she loves—coding and bunny rabbits. Her brother helped her make the game. Each time they played it, they found new ways to make it better. They made many different versions of the game. It took them more than a year to get it right.

The "CoderBunnyz" board game is set up like a farmyard adventure. The game is fun to play. It is also a great way to introduce kids to coding.

Samaira worked with professional **designers**. They helped her make her game look great. Her parents helped her find a company to make the game. By the time she was eight, CoderBunnyz was ready to sell!

CoderBunnyz was such a hit that Samaira made two more games.

- CoderMindz teaches kids about **artificial intelligence**, the ability of a machine to imitate intelligent human behavior.

- CoderMarz is about outer space and the planet Mars.

➡ **designer**—person who creates a new look or style for an item

Helping Other Kids

By the time Samaira was 11, she was selling three popular board games. She wanted to help even more kids learn to code. She started "Yes, One Billion Kids Can Code" to spread her love of coding across the world.

Samaira Mehta *(cont.)*

Helping Other Kids *(cont.)*

For every 20 games she sells, she donates a game. Her games go to libraries and schools around the world. Her goal is to get 1 billion kids into coding by the time she graduates from college. Not all these kids will work as coders when they grow up. But she knows that learning about coding makes kids better thinkers and problem solvers. Someday, these kids might help to solve big world problems.

Need Help Getting Started?

Samaira also wants to help kids start their own businesses. She started the "Boss Bizz" program to help. She used what she learned building her business as a model. Her program provides help in different ways:

- Samaira shows kids how to get a new business going step-by-step.
- Kids can hear from people who have built successful businesses.
- At the end, kids can **pitch** their ideas to win money to use for their ideas.

More Girls in Tech

Samaira knows that there are more men in **tech** jobs than women. She wants more girls to learn coding. She wants them to learn other STEM skills, too. She is working to get girls excited about STEM and computer science. She wants girls to grow up to be better thinkers. She wants girls to be leaders.

> "One of the biggest things that people can do to encourage women and girls in tech is to make them feel welcome in this field and make it more **inclusive** for girls. Just the simple things make a difference, like when you advertise a STEM or Robotics Club, show pictures of girls too."

Points of View

Kids and adults see things in different ways. Boys and girls can see things differently. People from different places see different things, too. It is important to have many **points of view** to solve the big problems of the world.

> ➠ **points of view**—ways of thinking and looking at the world

Name: ___________________________________ **Date:** ___________________

Key Ideas and Details

Directions: Answer the questions below about Samaira Mehta. Use complete sentences.

1. What is the main idea of this text?

   ____

   ____

   ____

2. Explain two ways Samaira works to get kids interested in coding.

   One: ____

   ____

   Two: ____

   ____

3. What does a *designer* do?

   ____

   ____

   Why do you think Samaira worked with designers on her board game?

   ____

   ____

Name: ________________________________ **Date:** _______________

Craft and Structure

Directions: Answer the questions below. Use complete sentences.

1. What does *coding* mean? Use the other words and sentences in the text to help you understand it.

   ____

   ____

2. Why do you think the author included the quotes from Samaira Mehta?

   ____

   ____

3. Choose one word from the text that you think is important to understand Samaira's story. Define the word, and explain its importance to the story.

   Word: ____

   Definition: ____

   ____

   Importance to the story: ________________________________

   ____

   ____

Name: _________________________________ **Date:** _______________

Integration of Knowledge and Meaning

Directions: Answer the questions below. Use complete sentences.

1. It took Samaira two years to create the CoderBunnyz game and get it ready to sell. Why do you think it took so long?

   ____

   ____

   Why do you think Samaira didn't give up?

   ____

   ____

2. Why did Samaira start "Yes, One Billion Kids Can Code"?

   ____

   ____

   Do you think she will meet her goal? Why or why not?

   ____

   ____

3. The text says: "It is important to have many points of view to solve the big problems of the world." What does this mean?

   ____

   ____

   Do you agree or disagree? Why?

   ____

   ____

Name: ________________________________ **Date:** ________________

Group Discussion

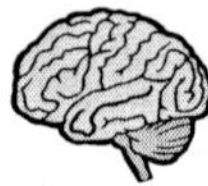 **Brainstorming:** Samaira Mehta loves computer coding. She works to help others learn to code. What do you love? How could you help others learn about it?

Taking Action

Choose a subject or skill that you care a lot about. Make a plan to share it.

Directions: Use this graphic organizer to make the plan.

My passion:

____

____

Why I love it:

____

____

What others need to know:

____

____

How I can help others learn about it:

____

____

Milo Cress

How Many Straws?

When Milo Cress was eight, he went to a restaurant with his family. He saw the server put a plastic straw in every drink. Milo didn't really need a straw. He looked around. Everyone had straws. He wondered how many plastic straws were used in the United States each day. He tried to figure it out, but he couldn't.

Milo decided to do his own research. He talked to the companies that made straws. He asked them how many they sell. He figured out that we use about 500 million straws every day! And that is just in the United States!

That number is so big that it can be hard to understand. Try to imagine 127 big, yellow school buses. Now picture them filled up with plastic straws. That is how many straws are used in restaurants, stores, schools, hospitals, and other places every day.

> "It seems extremely **wasteful** to make a product that we use for less than 15 minutes but that will be somewhere on Earth long after my own grandchildren are born."

Plastic Pollution

Think about what happens to a **disposable** plastic straw after you use it.

Usually, you throw it in the trash. What happens to our trash? Most of it gets buried in **landfills**.

- Things like banana peels or paper will **decompose**. They break down over time.

- Plastic straws and other plastic items do not decompose. They can last in the ground up to one thousand years!

Some plastic straws end up as **litter**.

- They get into rivers and oceans where they can hurt animals.

Plastic **pollution** is now found on every beach in the world. Scientists say that by the year 2050 there will be more plastic in the oceans than fish!

Milo Cress *(cont.)*

Be Straw Free

Milo started "Be Straw Free." He wants to help people make less plastic pollution. He asks restaurants to change. He wants them to *offer* straws to people instead of just giving them one. He asks people to say "no thank you" to straws if they don't need them. Some people need to use straws and that's okay. Milo just wants people to think about whether they really *need* a straw.

> **Think about this:** Nearly every bit of plastic that has ever been made is still around somewhere on Earth today.

Milo has a website where people can make a **pledge**. They promise not to use plastic straws for 30 days. People who take the pledge say it reminds them to do their part. It helps them think about things they can do to help the environment.

> "When I first started this project, I thought that adults wouldn't listen to what a kid has to say. I was wrong. Mayors in the United States and **abroad** as well as governors and congressmen listened. The National Restaurant Association was also willing to listen."
>
> ⇒ **abroad**—in a foreign country

Milo's "Be Straw Free" campaign was very successful:

- Milo's idea made people think about using less plastic.
- The governor of Colorado declared a Straw Free Day.
- The National Restaurant Association supports Milo's "offer first" policy.
- Now, Milo speaks at schools, restaurants, and other groups to spread the word.

> "Abraham Lincoln said that the best way to predict the future is to help create it. I think that's absolutely true. There's a lot that all of us can do to create a better future."

Name: _________________________________   **Date:** _________________

Key Ideas and Details

Directions: Answer the questions below about Milo Cress. Use complete sentences.

1. What problem did Milo Cress want to solve?

   ____

   Why? ____

   ____

2. Explain Milo's "offer first" idea for plastic straws.

   ____

   ____

   ____

   ____

3. What does *disposable* mean?

   ____

   ____

   List three items that are disposable.

   Item 1: ____

   Item 2: ____

   Item 3: ____

Name: _________________________________ **Date:** _______________

Craft and Structure

Directions: Answer the questions below. Use complete sentences.

1. What is *pollution*? Use context clues to help you understand it.

____

____

____

2. Why do you think the author included the quotes from Milo Cress?

____

____

3. Choose one word from the text that you think is important to understanding Milo's story. Define the word, and explain its importance to the story.

Word: ____

Definition: ____

____

Importance to the story: ______________________________________

____

____

Name: _________________________________   **Date:** _________________

Integration of Knowledge and Meaning

Directions: Answer the questions below. Use complete sentences.

1. Why is plastic *pollution* such a big problem?

   ____

   ____

   ____

2. Milo says that using so many straws is wasteful. What else do you think is *wasteful*?

   ____

   ____

   Why? ____

   ____

3. Think about all the trash you throw away every day. How could you make less trash?

   ____

   ____

   ____

Name: ______________________________ **Date:** ________________

Group Discussion

Brainstorming: Milo's "Be Straw Free" project tried to change people's behavior, or the way they act. Think about some things people do that you might like to ask them to change.

- ⌘ What are these behaviors?
- ⌘ What could people do instead?
- ⌘ How could you get people to change?

Taking Action

Choose a behavior you would like to get people to change.

Directions: Write the behavior you want to change and the new behavior you want people to do. Fill in the chart with convincing messages and ideas to spread the word.

Behavior I want to change: ________________________________

Behavior I want people to do instead: ________________________

Messages	Ways to Get the Word Out

Gitanjali Rao

Solving Problems with Science

Gitanjali Rao is busy. She is a good student. She swims and practices **fencing**. She plays piano. She practices Indian dancing and singing. She has also written and illustrated a book for kids. But her favorite thing to do is to solve problems.

Gitanjali is an **inventor**. She uses science and technology to help solve problems.

Inventions

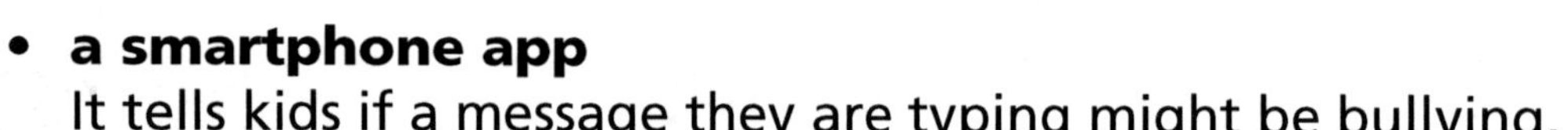

When she was in third grade, she heard about a water **crisis**. The drinking water in the city of Flint, Michigan was a problem. It had too much lead in it. Lead makes people sick. Gitanjali wanted to do something to help. She did research for four years on how to test for lead in water!

When she was 11, she invented a device that tests water. It works quickly and cheaply. It sends the results to a smartphone. Her invention can help people test their water easily to see if it is safe.

She keeps inventing new things. So far, she has invented:

- **a smartphone app**
  It tells kids if a message they are typing might be bullying.

- **a testing device for doctors**
  It tells doctors whether their patients are using dangerous drugs.

- **a snake bite detector**
  It tells people how bad a snake bite is. That way, they know if they need to get help fast.

She follows these steps when trying to solve a problem:

Observe—see what the problem is

Brainstorm—think of ways to fix the problem

Research—learn about the problem

Build—make something to solve the problem and test it until it works

Communicate—share ideas; work together to fix the problem

Have you used a process like this before?

Gitanjali Rao *(cont.)*

Inspiring Others to Innovate

Gitanjali wants to help other kids solve the world's problems. She wrote a book about innovation. It tells kids step-by-step how to turn an idea into reality.

She teaches classes to help kids learn to innovate. So far, she has taught over 46,000 students in more than ten countries! She wants to inspire others to try. She wants to show other kids that they can help, too.

> "If I can do it, you can do it, and anyone can do it."

Innovation

To **innovate** means to do something in a new way. People who innovate try new things. If one idea doesn't work, they try something else!

Here are some ways to practice innovation:

Build—Make things with paper, cardboard boxes, and other recycled materials. Try building the same idea in many different ways.

Play thinking games—Challenge your creative brain by asking, "What if…?"

Think about these ideas to get started:

- What if there was no gravity on the school playground? What would happen? What could you do?
- What if you could talk to animals?

Put things together—New ideas can come from putting things together that usually don't go together. For example, how are a moose and the moon connected? How about a watch and a marshmallow?

Let your mind wander—Sometimes, the best ideas come when you are not really thinking. Just let your mind go. See where it takes you!

> "I come up with some of my best ideas in the most generic (everyday) places. Sometimes they pop into my brain when I am swimming, pacing around my living room, or even just getting lemonade out of the refrigerator."

Name: _________________________________ **Date:** ________________

Key Ideas and Details

Directions: Answer the questions below about Gitanjali Rao. Use complete sentences.

1. What was the first problem Gitanjali Rao wanted to solve?

   ____

   ____

   How did she help?

   ____

   ____

2. What does *innovate* mean?

   ____

   ____

3. What do Gitanjali's inventions have in common?

   ____

   ____

   What are these inventions trying to do?

   ____

   ____

   Explain how one of Gitanjali's inventions works and who it can help.

   ____

   ____

   ____

Name: ___________________________   **Date:** ________________

Craft and Structure

Directions: Answer the questions below. Use complete sentences.

1. What is an *inventor*? Use context clues to help you understand it.

____

____

2. Why do you think the author included the quotes from Gitanjali Rao?

____

____

3. Choose one word from the text that you think is important to understanding Gitanjali's story. Define the word, and explain its importance to the story.

Word: ____

Definition: ______________________________________

____

Importance to the story: _________________________

____

____

Name: ________________________________   **Date:** ________________

Integration of Knowledge and Meaning

Directions: Answer the questions below. Use complete sentences.

1. Which of Gitanjali's inventions do you think could help the most people?

____

____

Why do you think so?

____

____

2. Reread the sidebar about innovation. Which idea would you like to try?

____

Why?

____

____

3. Why do you think Gitanjali wants to help other kids learn how to innovate?

____

____

____

Name: _______________________________   **Date:** _______________

Group Discussion

Brainstorming: Let's talk about it.

- ⌘ What inventions do you use every day?
- ⌘ How do these inventions make your life better?
- ⌘ What new inventions would you like to see?
- ⌘ How would each idea help you or help others?

Taking Action

Choose a problem in your community. Think about how a new invention could help. For example, if there is litter all over your school playground, could you invent something to quickly pick up the litter and sort it into trash and recycling?

Directions: Write about your invention idea. Don't worry if you don't know how to build it yet. Just write about what you would do if you could!

What is your innovative idea?

____

Draw a sketch of your invention.

How does your invention work?

____

____

____

How will your invention help others?

____

____

____

Motto Bookmarks

Kids Taking Action

"There's a lot that all of us can do to create a better future."

—Milo Cress

Kids Taking Action

"Don't give up. Give back!"

—Scheinman Family Motto

Kids Taking Action

"If I can do it, you can do it, and anyone can do it."

—Gitanjali Rao

Kids Taking Action

"Somebody needs help? Just go and do it."

—Hana Fatima

Kids Taking Action

"I want to tell the whole world that everyone is equal."

—Jane Velkovski

Kids Taking Action

"Don't wait to be great!"

—Jahkil Naeem Jackson

Kids Taking Action

"Kids can change the world. So, let's do it now!"

—Hailey Scheinman

Bibliography

Unit 1: Christian Bucks

Bucks, Justin. (2018, December 3). Buddy Bench turns 5: York Co. dad's tribute to son who started national kindness movement. York Daily Record. https://www.ydr.com/story/opinion/2018/12/03/buddy-bench-turns-5-christian-bucks-dad-offers-tribute-his-son/2190041002/.

Scherker, Amanda. 2nd Grader's Cure for Playground Loneliness: A Buddy Bench. (12/03/2013;updated December 6, 2017) https://www.huffpost.com/entry/second-grader-buddy-bench_n_4378248.

Unit 2: Aiden Wang

Kim, Hye-Jin. (2021, June 21; updated 2022, January 11) The butterfly whisperer: 11-year-old lepidopterist is subject of new documentary. Community News. https://www.communitynews.org/towns/west-windsor-plainsboro-news/the-butterfly-whisperer-11-year-old-lepidopterist-is-subject-of-new-documentary/article_d5a14109-a085-5261-bd33-22223c617e5e.html.

Skelly, Richard. (2020, April 1). Wang builds Monarch butterfly movement in central N.J. American Farm Publications. https://americanfarmpublications.com/wang-builds-monarch-butterfly-movement-in-central-n-j/.

Unit 3: Garrett Lowry

Pellott, Emerald. (2016, June 21) 10-Year-Old Secretly Knits Caps for Needy Kids. https://littlethings.com/lifestyle/hats-for-kids.

Wilson, Alley. (2016, June 26) 10-year-old knits hats for kids in hospital because he wants them to know they're 'loved'. https://globalnews.ca/news/2788275/10-year-old-knits-hats-for-kids-in-hospital-because-he-wants-them-to-know-theyre-loved/.

Unit 4: A'Layah Robinson

Miller, Anthony. (2017, April 18) Oklahoma girl raises money for foster kids. https://www.kxii.com/content/news/Oklahoma-girl-raises-money-for-foster-kids-419700763.html.

Troxtell, Adam. (2017, March 14). Six-year-old's lemonade sales provide supplies to foster children. CNHI, LLC. https://www.cnhi.com/featured_stories/six-year-olds-lemonade-sales-provide-supplies-to-foster-children/article_ee3c0a04-08f8-11e7-9e61-7f1c50485ee9.html.

Unit 5: Hailey Scheinman

Hofstaedter, Maggie. Hailey Scheinman—Don't Give Up. Give Back! https://inspiremykids.com/hailey-scheinman-taking-sisterly-love-to-a-whole-new-level/.

Ivanhoe Newswire. (2020, August 30). Kids Crew: Hailey connects kids of all abilities. WPSD Local 6. https://www.wpsdlocal6.com/news/kids-crew-hailey-connects-kids-of-all-abilities/article_5c06dc9e-eb2c-11ea-aa54-f32b0a7c5d82.html.

Ramos, Jillian. (2020, March 20). Move over Marvel: Clearwater has their very own teenage superhero. WFTS. https://www.abcactionnews.com/news/region-pinellas/move-over-marvel-clearwater-has-their-very-own-teenage-superhero.

Bibliography *(cont.)*

Unit 6: Hana Fatima

Colpitts, Iain. (2021, April 20). 9-year-old from Mississauga inspires others to volunteer in community. Totonto Star. https://www.thestar.com/local-mississauga/life/2021/04/20/9-year-old-from-mississauga-inspires-others-to-volunteer-in-community.html.

Nasser, Shanifa. (updated 2021, April 9). Meet the 9-year-old girl whose simple act of kindness during COVID-19 spurred an army of volunteers. CBC News. https://www.cbc.ca/news/canada/toronto/covid-kindness-good-neighbour-project-hana-fatima-1.5980113.

Unit 7: Jane Velkovski

sportanddev.org. (2017, August 21). "I will be a footballer, I will score goals like Ronaldo". https://www.sportanddev.org/en/article/news/i-will-be-footballer-i-will-score-goals-ronaldo.

UEFA.com. (updated 2017, December 15). "When I play football, I feel like everyone else." UEFA.com. https://www.uefa.com/insideuefa/about-uefa/news/023f-0f8e59792f15-7818c9a3ec29-1000--when-i-play-football-i-feel-like-everyone-else/.

Unit 8: Jakhil Naeem Jackson

Jackson, Jakhil Naeem. Making a Choice to Make a Difference https://magazine.thestriveproject.com/issue/oct-dec-2020/making-a-choice-to-make-a-difference/.

Wiedmann, Corrie, & Wondercratekids. (2019, July 14). Kids Making a Difference: Jahkil Naeem Jackson, Founder of Project i AM. Wonder Crate. https://www.wondercratekids.com/2019/07/14/kids-making-a-difference-jahkil-naeem-jackson-founder-of-project-i-am/.

Unit 9: Samaira Mehta

I am Generation Equality: Samaira Mehta, champion for girls in technology. (2020, April 23) UN Women. https://www.unwomen.org/en/news/stories/2020/4/i-am-generation-equality-samaira-mehta-champion-for-girls-in-technology.

Sofat, Alyssa. (2020, July 9). Samaira Mehta, Founder, CoderBunnyz: Santa Clara, California. The Fem Word. https://www.thefemword.world/her-story/samaira-mehta-coderbunnyz.

Unit 10: Milo Cress

Bailey, K. (n.d.). Meet Milo, founder of Be Straw Free. Ecocycle. https://www.ecocycle.org/bestrawfree/about.

The Last Straw — Milo Cress. https://www.youngvoicesfortheplanet.com/the-last-straw-milo-cress/.

Unit 11: Gitanjali Rao

Stutman, Michael. Gitanjali Rao - Time's First Kid of the Year — "If I Can Do It, You Can Do It!". InspireMyKids. (2021, February 3). https://inspiremykids.com/gitanjali-rao-times-first-kid-of-the-year-if-i-can-do-it-you-can-do-it/.